Judgment Authority · First Edition

Xiaoqing Wang

Copyright and Rights

Judgment Authority · First Edition

ISBN: 979-8-9947559-0-7
Published by Judgment Authority Press
Publication date: 2026-01-29

Edition Status

This First Edition is frozen as the authoritative reference for the Judgment Authority framework.

This document constitutes the original published reference of the Judgment Authority framework.

How to Cite

Use of the term "Judgment Authority" in a definitional or structural sense to describe systems, products, or services implies reference to this publication as the original definition source, unless otherwise stated.

When referencing this work, use the following citation format:

Xiaoqing Wang. *Judgment Authority*. First Edition, 2026.

Contents

1 Judgment Authority

1.1 Original Definition Anchor

First Edition

(Original publication of the Judgment Authority framework)

This text defines the original structure, language, and boundaries of the Judgment Framework, and constitutes the sole original definition of Judgment as used in this framework.

It is published as a reference document.

Rights and Usage Boundary

This First Edition defines the original structure, terminology, and boundaries of the Judgment Authority framework.

Reading, discussion, and citation are permitted. When citing, reference this work as the original definition source.

Reproducing substantial portions of this text, or reusing the framework as an integrated system in products, services, automation, training materials, or commercial operations without authorization is not permitted.

Implementation details (including APIs, schemas, protocols, and SDKs) are intentionally not included in this edition. Any implementation that presents itself as based on this framework should preserve attribution and respect the boundary between definition and application.

This notice does not constitute a trademark claim, and does not restrict descriptive or referential use of the term outside a definitional or structural context.

2 Scope and Non-Scope

2.1 Scope

Judgment is the act of determining whether a given structure remains valid for continued participation.

Judgment evaluates structural validity only.

2.2 Non-Scope

Judgment does not provide execution guidance, optimization paths, improvement strategies, or outcome guarantees.

Judgment exists independently of results.

3 What Judgment Is

3.1 Definition

Judgment is a structural determination, not a behavioral recommendation.

3.2 Structural Nature

Judgment evaluates structural conditions, not intentions, efforts, promises, or competence.

3.3 Completion Without Action

Judgment is complete at the moment a verdict is reached, regardless of whether the verdict is acted upon.

4 What Judgment Is Not

Judgment is not decision-making.

Judgment is not optimization.

Judgment is not problem-solving.

Judgment is not negotiation.

Judgment is not prediction.

Judgment is not execution.

5 Judgment Vocabulary

5.1 STOP

STOP indicates that continuation is structurally invalid.

5.2 CONTINUE

CONTINUE indicates that continuation remains structurally valid.

5.3 REVIEW

REVIEW indicates that available structural information is insufficient for judgment.

5.4 UNDETERMINED

UNDETERMINED indicates that judgment is suspended due to insufficient structural information.

6 Judgment Structure

6.1 Overview

Judgment is expressed through a fixed structural order. This order is not interchangeable.

6.2 Signal

A Signal is a detectable structural condition indicating potential invalidity or stress.

6.3 Mechanism

A Mechanism is the causal structure by which a signal affects system integrity.

6.4 Consequence

A Consequence is the unavoidable result if continuation proceeds under the identified mechanism.

6.5 Boundary

A Boundary is the limit beyond which participation transfers risk or responsibility.

6.6 Verdict

A Verdict is the structural conclusion derived from the preceding elements.

6.7 Order Invariance

The structural order of judgment must be preserved.

7 Responsibility and Authority

7.1 Responsibility Retention

Responsibility for continuation always remains with the acting individual or organization.

7.2 Non-Transferability

Responsibility cannot be transferred, absorbed, or neutralized by structure, role, or process.

7.3 Delegation Without Ownership

Judgment analysis may be delegated. Responsibility may not.

8 Prohibited Interpretations

The following prohibitions are normative and standalone. Each applies independently and must be interpreted without contextual extension.

8.1 No Prediction

Judgment does not predict outcomes.

8.2   No Optimization

Judgment does not optimize systems.

8.3 No Moral Evaluation

Judgment does not assign moral value.

8.4 No Execution Instruction

Judgment does not instruct execution.

9 Reference Status Declaration

9.1 Original Publication

This text defines the original published structure and language of the Judgment Framework.

9.2 Authority Boundary

This publication serves as a reference boundary, not as an operational system.

The rights and usage boundary for this framework is explicitly defined within this publication.

9.3 Derivative Works

All subsequent interpretations, implementations, or systems are derivative and non-authoritative.

9.4 Non-Operational Nature

The Judgment Framework exists to define limits, not to perform actions.

Judgment Authority is a framework about judgment boundaries, decision legitimacy, and responsibility allocation.

This First Edition presents the original formulation without interpretation or adaptation.

The text is intentionally minimal and structural.

www.ingramcontent.com/pod-product-compliance
Lightning Source LLC
Chambersburg PA
CBHW040931210326
41597CB00030B/5266